Think About It!

The Griot/umbono Series

Think About It!

The Question Book For Those Curious About Race

Ronald L. Jackson II, Ph.D.

Writers Club Press

San Jose New York Lincoln Shanghai

Think About It!
The Question Book For Those Curious About Race

Writers Club Press
an imprint of iUniverse.com, Inc.

For information address:
iUniverse.com, Inc.
620 North 48th Street, Suite 201
Lincoln, NE 68504-3467
www.iuniverse.com

ISBN: 0-595-14231-1

Printed in the United States of America

To my son Niles
whose thirst for knowledge flows like a river

Contents

Acknowledgements

First, I must thank God who is the head of my life and as master of all things created, brought forth all existence through the power of the spoken word. Naturally, the word gives life to knowledge and inspiration to creativity.

I am grateful for the unflinching support from my loving mother Sharon Marie Prather, my wonderful wife and soul mate Ricci, and my two beautiful children Niyah and Niles. A special thanks goes to my intellectual sparring partners and best male friends Bruce (my brother), Brad, Lawrence, Theo, Carlos, Keith and Shaun. I must also acknowledge and thank my father Ron Sr. and stepmom Georgie, as well as my little brother and sister Tishaun and Tita. Each of you mentioned here have been inspirational and supportive and to that extent have expanded my life.

I also thank my students and colleagues (who kept me on the right track) at Howard University, University of the District of Columbia, Xavier University, Shippensburg University and Penn State University.

Additionally, I am thankful for the warm way in which this book was received by those who endorsed it—Drs. Veronica Duncan, Keith Wilson, James Stewart, Brenda J. Allen, Mark McPhail, Aaron Gresson, Bryan Wade, and Kathy Brooks.

Last, but not least, I must express my gratitude to the publisher of this book, IUniverse, for their patience, diligence, and enthusiasm.

Introduction

Think About It! is a book of questions for those who are just plain curious. It is different than any other question book on the market because of two features—inspirational and humorous quotations and easily accessible chapters. Many people are inquisitive and just as many are searching for the truth within personal relationships and several other places as well. For example, every religion has an interpretation of truth. Every school, business, family and loving relationship has a perspective. The fact is, many people turn to others to find the truth when ultimately, the real truth is within each of us. It is others who facilitate that discovery. This is not to say that we as individuals have all of life's answers, but that we must make the final decisions concerning the direction in which our lives will go. So, when reading *Think About It!* don't get "hung up" on getting the answers right. That is not the point. The point is to think about why you answered as you did and what that says about you. Ask yourself if you think you will eventually change your answers and what experiences led to your present answers. Self-discovery is key!

Think About It! was written over a period of seven years and is a result of having read other question books that I felt inadequately addressed my cultural consciousness and quenched my intellectual thirst. I have carefully written and rewritten each question in order to broaden your exploration as you read. Initially, it took six months to complete, but I spent the remaining six years or so test marketing the book in college classes and among business executives, friends, colleagues and family members. Every time I introduce the book in conversations, the discussions are fun, lively and I admit sometimes intense, but always interesting. After several years of hosting mini "think tanks," noone has ever left the conversation upset. As a matter of fact, people do not want to put the book down. There is never a dull moment. Beware: conversations may last for hours!

Carry *Think About It!* along with you when you are out of town for business or pleasure. Take it with you to work and read it during your break or to the salon while waiting to get your hair done. You may even want to take it to church for a "singles" or "couples" day or to a family or friendly gathering. Maybe you are a professor or cultural trainer like me and may find it useful in your classrooms or during training sessions. Perhaps, you will just carry it along while eating ice cream on a sunny day. It is portable and easy to read.

This is not a book to sit down and read in one sitting and then shelve among the other books in your library. Keep *Think About It!* on the coffee table or nightstand where it is easily accessible so that you can revisit and reanswer questions with ease. Keep a journal or try to remember if your perspectives change either over time or after hearing responses from your friends and family.

Remember: Many of the questions that are culture-specific can be asked of other cultures as well, so feel free to substitute words.

Two Ways to Enjoy Think About It!

While there are multiple ways in which *Think About It!* can be used, there are two suggestions for games that can be played with friends using *Think About It!* Before explaining the details of the games, there are some basic ground rules that must be followed. All except 3 and 4 also apply to you when you are alone.

1. Be honest with yourself and other players. Give yourself permission to ask and answer the hard questions, the uncomfortable ones.
2. Be mature about your answers and self-monitoring.

3. Be fair when listening to others and do not attack them for not agreeing with you!
4. Respect and be sensitive to others' concerns and issues. We all have them.
5. Take ownership for how you feel. Do not disown your thoughts by saying things like "Everybody thinks..." or "People tend to believe..."
6. Have Fun!!!

Game #1: Think Tank (two versions for groups)

Three or more players are required. Tell them you want to introduce a game where complete honesty is key. Even if you feel you can't be honest with the group, be honest with yourself. Everyone is a winner in these games. The games are not set up so that the content of one's answers can be wrong.

Version One

In the first version of "think tank" each person selects a page number. Or, you may choose a category/chapter first (Family, Mind, Body, & Spirit, All About You, Love & Relationships, Race, Color & Liberation, Right or Wrong? or That's Deep) and then randomly select a page number. Once selected, read the question aloud and allow each person to truthfully respond after taking no more than 60 seconds to think about the question. Then, converse naturally. Ask each other to explain answers and clarify what is not fully understood. Interpret the question strictly as written. If the question still seems ambiguous, share your individual interpretations of the question and your answers.

Version Two

In version two of "think tank" each person will be given a sheet of paper and a pen. Each sheet of paper must be the same size and color and each pen must have the same color ink. There shall be no unique or identifying marks on the paper including names, artwork or folds. Number the paper one to ten. Sit in a circle and pass the book around from person to person giving each individual a chance to select a question of interest. (If you only have one copy of the book, you may choose to randomly select a page number to save time rather than waiting until each person has skimmed all of the questions.) Once selected, indicate the page number and read the question aloud. Each person must write a response to the question in the order in which the questions are read. They have two minutes to think about and write a response to the question.

Be sure to designate at least one person to keep track of the question page numbers and the order in which they are read for the group. Of course, in small groups, the book will circulate more than once or twice. You might even want to number the page so that every person is given a chance to read the same number of questions (e.g. 3/person). Once all questions have been read and all answers are recorded, then place all sheets face down in the middle of the circle and jumble them up. Once mixed up, then everyone, one-by-one must close their eyes and reach into the pile and pick a sheet. If you get your own sheet, then redo the jumbling. Every person should have someone else's sheet.

The one who bought the book should be the facilitator or designate someone to take on that role. The facilitator will go back to each question in the order that they were read, and reread the question. For example, once the question is reread, the facilitator says, "The answer on the sheet I have says..." or "This person answered..." Thereafter, every person shares the answer to that question on the sheet in front of him or her. After all questions and answers are read consecutively, the group must try to guess whose sheets they have in front of them. Start with the person to the right of the facilitator and go around the circle. That person identifies the person by name. If the guess is incorrect, the facilitator shall ask for any other guesses. Do not go on to the next sheet until someone in the group has correctly guessed. By simple process of elimination, someone will guess correctly and that person is the next to guess whose paper is in front of him or her. After everyone is figured out, the game ends.

Game #2: Pillow Talk (for couples)

Unlike "think tank" where you are encouraged to read and reflect on multiple questions in a small or large group, the object of pillow talk is for two companions or lovers to select a few questions and reflect more intensely. Remember to have fun! Still, be honest and don't be afraid to answer questions that challenge your perspective. The idea is to learn more about what makes your partner tick. Sometimes in relationships or friendships, people forget to ask questions about personal philosophies or life orientations. Take this opportunity to carefully select three questions each. Choose questions that you *really* would like to know the answers to, not just ones that are interesting or non-confrontative. Remember: confrontation does not have to be negative. Also, keep in mind that the purpose of "pillow talk" is NOT to interrogate viciously or attack; it is to grow as a loving couple or as friends by getting to know each other better. So, grab your favorite beverage and prepare your favorite snack. Most of all have a nice time!!!

Race, Color, & Liberation

Racism

Would you rather work and live around people who were blatantly racist
or those who seemed
nice, but were hiding their racist views?

Do White-Americans experience racism? Explain.

Can Blacks be racist? Why or why not?

Racial Slurs & Remarks

"There can be no union between slavery and freedom"
(H. Ford Douglas)

Have you ever dismissed a blatant racial slur without responding?

Would you say anything if your superior made an insulting joke/remark about your race?
(e.g. referring to Blacks as "you people")

Are racial jokes ever acceptable to you? Does it make a difference who's telling the joke?

Race Consciousness

"When we speak of peace, we must also speak of freedom."
(Angela Y. Davis)

Do you feel that race pride and consciousness
contribute to the destruction or success of our youth?

Are you more likely to invite a Black or White co-worker
to dinner (assuming both are peers of yours) and why?

Do you ever feel disgusted by the amount of racial progress made by
African Americans?

Separation & Integration

"Introduce me to a world where I don't have to miss myself."
(Leslie Reese)

Which do you think will lead Blacks to liberation first, separatism or integration? Explain

Have you ever been the only person of color in a class, boardroom, or organization?
How did that experience effect you, if at all?

Do you feel most comfortable with neighbors who are Black or non-Black? Explain.

Language & Culture

"Naming is an incantation, a creative act....Every word is an effective word, every word is binding....Every word has consequences."
(Janheinz Jahn)

Considering the diversity within cultures, is there really any such thing as sounding White or Black?

How do you feel about Black people who change their names to African names?
How is their success in the workplace effected?

Should the word "nigger" or "niggah" be eliminated from the vocabulary of African Americans?

Gender & Maturity

"People tend to fear the thing they want the most."
(Author Unknown)

Is manhood judged by freedom or responsibility?

Should your children be taught about culture at home or is culture just a lived experience?

Defining Culture

"Nothing pains some people more than having to think."
(M.L. King, Jr.)

Are you born into a culture or is it learned?

Is there any significant difference between race, ethnicity and culture?
Or, are these terms all the same?

If you were asked to describe the American culture, what would you say?

Freedom of Cultural Expression

"None of us are free until all of us are free."
(Kwame Nkrumah)

Do you feel you have complete freedom in your life? If not, will you ever?

Is "playing the dozens" constructive or destructive behavior?

Do Whites negotiate or adjust their identities when they come in contact with Blacks?

Legends, Myths, & Heroes

"You are the sum total of all your beliefs, and your beliefs are always subject to change as your knowledge base expands."
(Anthony Browder)

Who are your cultural heroes/sheroes and why?

Should the African American community support an African American political candidate just because he/she is African American? Should we have this approach toward supporting Black businesses?

Is it necessary, in terms of liberation, for African Americans to believe that Jesus was a particular color?

Race & Achievement

"To say that all Whites are racist is to say that all grass is green,
and everything that's green is grass."
(Maya Angelou)

Is racism unavoidable for Blacks in America?

Do you think that your skin color, gender, or race
prevent you from achieving your fullest potential?

Who do you think is responsible for racism?

Issues that unify & divide the Black community

"The revolution will not be televised."
(Gil Scott Heron)

Fact or fiction: If you want to hide something
from Blacks, put it in a book?
How do we teach our children that it's cool,
and not "nerdy" to be intellectual ?

Are efforts like the million man march remedying the problem in the
Black community, or simply putting a "band-aid" on them?

What is the key to uniting the Black family?

Racial Preference

"It's a dog-eat-dog world, and I'm wearing milkbone shorts."
(Kelly Allen)

Do you think that other "minorities"
are treated better than African Americans are?

In your opinion, should hate groups like the KKK be
given the right to hold public demonstrations?

In the case of Susan Smith (the woman
who killed her children and blamed it on a Black
man), if she had been a Black woman blaming
a White man, do you think the
media would have responded in the same way? What about the police?

Human Differences

"Our young must be taught that racial peculiarities do exist,
but that beneath the skin,
beyond the differing textures...we are more
alike my friend, than we are unalike."
(Maya Angelou)

Is it better to discuss racism with your kids before or after they experience racism? Or not at all?

Do you believe Whites have a different sense of humor than Blacks?

At the core, are all humans really the same?

Contextualizing Culture

"Culture shapes behavior. We cannot escape it. Even Jesus was a Jew."
(Maulana Karenga)

Do you believe that a person's environment or
socioeconomic status shapes their behavior?

Is it necessary to claim membership in a certain culture
or is it okay to just be human? What if you
are the product of more than one cultural lineage,
do you claim all or just the dominant one?

Does it really make a difference what Blacks call themselves
(i.e. Black, African American, Colored, Negro, etc.) ?

Cultural Diversity

"I am because we are, and because we are, I am."
(John Mbiti)

Is it possible for humans to exist without culture?

Do you feel that cultural diversity has become a fad?
If it did not effect business profits,
would it still be a concern to American businesses?

Do you think that race relations are improved by having
cross-cultural relationships and/or friendships?

Color-Blindness

"I believe that most of the limitations we have are self-imposed."
(Les Brown)

Do issues of skin color still divide the Black community everywhere we are?

Do sports promote color-blindness? (i.e. the belief
that one does not notice color when looking
at another person) Is the cure for racism in not seeing color ?

Does your perception of beauty or preference in intimate partners
have anything to do with skin color?

Black Shame &
Embarrassment

"Black people cannot avoid the critical questions:
Who am I? Am I who I say I am? And, am I all I ought to be?"
(Maulana Karenga quoting Frantz Fanon)

Have you ever wished you were part of another culture?
If your complexion was such that you were able to be mistaken as
being part of another culture, would you pretend that you actually were?

What behavior among people who are members of your culture
embarrasses you? What behavior makes you proud?

Right or Wrong
(Ethical Dilemmas)

Gender & Equality

"No matter how full the river is, it still wants to grow."
(Proverb of Zaire)

Does demanding gender equality involve the elimination of chivalry?

Do you consider all-female or all-male academies discriminatory institutions?

Is there any situation in which it is appropriate for a man to hit a woman?

Censorship/Monitoring Others

"One falsehood spoils a thousand truths."
(Ashanti Proverb)

Should music with sexually explicit lyrics be valued for
its directness or criticized for its vulgarity?

In your opinion, what is the worst thing you can teach a child?

Do you think that the Black community
should rear an elite group that is designed
to monitor, infiltrate and eliminate White organizations
that are a threat to the Black community?

Racial Injustice & Solutions

"It is easier to wrap ourselves in dozens of virtues than to admit a single fault."
(Unknown Author)

Is it wrong to expect reparations from 20th and 21st century Whites for the oppression that their forefathers inflicted on Blacks?

Is being angry about oppression counterproductive or productive?

If you could go anywhere in time and alter the course of events, but your privilege would cost an innocent person their life, would you do it? If so, where would you go?

Ethics & American Politics

"Democracy is the name we give to the people when we need them."
(Robert Pellevé)

Do you think that it is ethical for the government to regulate
the number of children born to each family?

Is there a better system of government than democracy
for the United States? If so, which one?

Does the government respond differently to White militant
organizations than Black militant organizations?

Race, Ethics, & Honor

"Sin is geographical."
(Bertrand Russell)

If you could kill someone you didn't like
and get away with it, would you do it?

If you invented a cure for AIDS and you were given
the privilege to market it to any community first,
which would it be and why? What price would you put on it?

Are race-based scholarships unethical?

Defining what is right

"The Tao that can be named is not the infinite Tao."
(Tao Teh Ching)

What is your definition of ethics?

Is there such thing as a white lie? Is it less significant than any other lie?

Real experiences, real choices

"Money isn't everything. The individual has to live with the choices they make."
(Sharon Prather)

If you were a lawyer and your client confided in you
that he was guilty of murder, but he paid you
a million dollars to continue to represent him, would you do it?

If you were an employer with two applicants (one Black and
one White) for a senior management position, both equally
qualified, would race make a difference in your decision?

Suppose you are a government agent who has been asked to arrest a citizen who fought for a cause you secretly believed in, what would you do?

Tempering Justice

"You cannot fix what you will not face."
(James Baldwin)

Suppose you have some information that could change the entire outlook of society for the better, but it would cause massive civil chaos in the meantime, would you release the information?

If you could reverse the roles Blacks and Whites play
in the perpetuation of capitalism, would you want to do it?
Would you inflict racism upon Whites out of revenge?

Would you die to save a thousand people? What if they were members of the KKK who promised to change their lives if you saved them?

Personal Moral Decisions

"Truth is the safest lie."
(Unknown)

Do you think it is wrong for a person to
ignore traffic signals at night when noone is looking?

Is it wrong for a person to have sex with a prostitute?

Do you think that physician-assisted suicide is wrong?

Parent-Child Relations

*"Some kids do what you say. Some kids do what you say
not to do. But all kids do what you do."*
(Unknown Author)

Should a child be allowed to reject parental authority or decision making?

Should you spank your child? If not, what other
disciplinary measures are appropriate to use?

At what age should children be encouraged to get a job?

Social Issues & Ethics

"I am here to live out loud."
(Emile Zola)

Should Black children be taught not to speak Black English?

Are athletes paid too much?

Why do you suppose that educators are not paid as much as athletes?
Is it that their jobs are not as important?

Love & Attraction

"The fool speaks, the wise man listens."
(Ethiopian Proverb)

If you could, would you marry more than one companion?

If your spouse was no longer capable of
being fertile and you wanted children,
how would you cope or wouldn't you?

If someone you were very attracted to, confided in you that he/she had
no ambitions/goals in life, but just wanted to live, how would you
respond? Would you still be interested?

Good Parenting

"Values spring from the seeds of encouragement."
(Anonymous)

Should parents pay their children for good grades?

Should children be given allowance? Up until what age?

Should children be made to believe in Santa Claus, The Easter Bunny, The Tooth Fairy, and other fictional characters?

Thinking Back, Thinking Black

"I always wanted to be somebody, but I should have been more specific."
(Lily Tomlin & Jane Wagner)

Do you believe in capital punishment?

When discussing African American culture,
are you talking about something that applies to all
African Americans or just a portion of the community?

Who decides whether you are Black? If you are Black and you
say that you are White, does that make it so?

Violence & Death

"Some people say it takes courage to face the matter of death....
I believe it takes more courage to face life."
(J. California Cooper)

Is it wrong to avenge the death of a loved one
by killing the one who murdered him/her?

Is there any instance in which you would kill for a family member?
What about an instance in which you would die for them?

Politics of Race

"Everything is political."
(P. Eric Abercrumbie)

Is affirmative action unfair?

Do you think that the Black church
should have a role in electoral politics?

What is your standard for determining who is a "sell-out" to the race?

The Family

Childrearing

"Our move is back toward the extended family, back toward the humanistic involvement of families with families.... The basis of our family, as is our struggle, is love."
(Haki Madhubuti)

Should the African American community
return to the days of communal childrearing?

Is it necessary for husbands and wives to
agree on childrearing practices and techniques?

Are girls and boys reared differently in Black families?

Defining Gender Identity

"It is the fool that is thirsty in the midst of water"
(Ethiopian Proverb)

Do you believe that Black women are more mature
than Black men are? Why or why not?

Is it okay for a female to actively pursue a male she finds attractive?

Is it appropriate for females to propose marriage to the one they love?

Black Family

"To the extent that Blacks forsake the family and the role they must play in it, the greater their vulnerability....The family represents the basic collectivization of the Black community and contains within it the potential for Black survival" *(Robert Staples)*

Is there such thing as a typical Black family?

Is it important that families sit down and dine together?

Describe the ideal Black family.

Marriage

"Love is an extension of the self. It should be defined as conscious unity."
(Bradford Hogue)

What is the key to an everlasting marriage in your opinion?

Are there any conditions under which extramarital affairs are justifiable?

Do you have the same feelings about homosexual and
heterosexual marriage and divorce?

Parenting

"A parent is the one who raises you."
(Anonymous)

How would you react if your 14 year-old daughter
told you she was pregnant?

Is it necessary to physically discipline your child?

What one thing did your parents teach you that you remember the most?

Family Planning

"You can't get to know better days unless you make it through the night."
(Tony Lorrich)

At what age should young couples begin to plan for retirement?

If you had the choice, would you want
to have twins, triplets, or quadruplets?

Do you think that only Blacks should adopt Black children?

Life Decisions

"Without life, there is nothing"
(Zulu Proverb)

Should all persons, regardless of age, begin writing a will?

If a very close loved one was in the hospital, near death, unable to speak or write, and in pain, do you feel that you have the right to "pull the plug."

Only Children

"Train a child up in the way [s]he should go and when
[s]he is old, [s]he will not depart from it"
(Holy Bible—Proverbs 22:6)

Is it true that the average "only child" is spoiled rotten?

Do you think that a husband and wife should have more
than one child, one child, or none?

Centralizing the Family Role

"Courage isn't having the strength to go on,
but going on when you do not have the strength"
(Anonymous author)

Are shows like "The Cosby Show" and "Parenthood"
unrealistic in their portrayal of the Black family?

Should parents teach their daughters to be aggressive?

When does a man/woman become a man/woman?

Black Church

"One who stands for nothing will fall for anything"
(Unknown author)

Should young children be given an option
as to whether they will attend church?

Should Black families attend Black churches or does it make a difference?

Family relationships

"Life is too short to live on the margin"
(R.L. Jackson, II)

What do you think about adults who
still live at home with their healthy parents?

Do you feel compelled to do more
to celebrate mother's day than father's day?

If a family member was in an abusive relationship,
do you feel obligated to intervene? If so, when?

Growing Up/Maturity & Guidance

"If you're not a part of the solution, then you're part of the problem"
(Eldridge Cleaver)

When is the appropriate time to
discuss the "Birds & the Bees" with your child?

How do you raise a child to be independent,
ambitious, and selfless? If neither you or
your mate exhibit these qualities can this be done?

How does being raised by homosexual parents effect children?

Cultural Consciousness

"Being Black is not a color, it's an experience"
(Kathy Russell)

Would you ever marry someone outside your culture?

Should all Black families celebrate
Kwanzaa and dispense with Christmas?

Do you encourage your family to buy Black-owned products and support
Black-owned businesses? Do you support them yourself?

Family Matters/Directions

*"No one individual builds anything; an individual may have had an
idea, but to see the fruition of the idea, you need collective action"*
(Haki Madhubuti)

Is there always a parent who emerges as the leader in the family?

Who is the person most responsible for who you are today?

Is it ever okay to disown a family member?

Loving You

*"One can neither grow mentally nor emotionally if they
choose to cultivate isolation rather than intimacy."
(Lawrence Anderson)*

Is it important, in your opinion, for you
and your mate to maintain an active sex life after sixty?

How well do you know your mate?
(i.e. favorite scent, song, artist, color, book, etc.)

The Man in the Family

*"Men, first of all, must define themselves. When you
define yourself, that's a declaration of manhood."*
(Na'im Akbar)

Is there a difference between Black masculinity and Black manhood?

How do you feel about men being househusbands? Is it okay?

Coping with Divorce

"One can imitate only one thing—reality"
(James Baldwin)

Do you feel it is necessary for a couple
to stay together for the sake of a child?

Do you think that children of single-parent
households think and behave
Differently than those reared in dual-parent households?

Coping with Family Challenges

"There comes a time when silence is betrayal."
(Martin Luther King, Jr.)

How do you handle a family member who attempts
to do drugs in your house, in your presence?

If a family member committed a crime, and wanted to hide out
at your place, would you allow them to do so?

Should families force children to go to college,
or should it be the child's choice?

Mind, Body & Spirit

Religion & You

"If one has not found something for which he will die, then
he is not fit to live."
(Martin Luther King, Jr.)

Is there any cause for which you would die?

Which biblical character best represents who you are?

Is there a difference between being religious and spiritual?

After Life

"Never have I not existed... and never in the future shall we cease to exist."
(Bhagavad Gita)

Is there such thing as heaven and hell or do people just die?

Do you think you realize whether you're in heaven
or hell when you die? Why do
you suppose people are preoccupied with images of heaven and hell?

Do you believe in reincarnation?

Psychics

*"A little knowledge misused is dangerous; a great amount
of knowledge not used properly is criminal."*
(Haki Madhubuti)

Have you or would you ever consult a psychic?

Do psychics misuse their gifts for monetary gain?

What is the difference between psychics, prophets, and angels?
Are they all the same or is one the devil?

Karma

"The end is in the beginning which lies far ahead"
(Ralph Ellison)

Does everything really happen for a reason?
If so, how do you explain slavery?

Do you believe that all humans are predestined to meet
certain persons and do certain things in this life while on earth?
Does that make God a dictator or a just ruler?

Do you believe that the universe is well ordered? (i.e. what goes
around comes back around)

Looking Ahead/The Future

"Have you ever asked yourself why is it that
we don't control the space which we occupy?"
(Haki Madhubuti)

Do you believe that even after the physical body
has decayed, the spirit lives on?

Do you believe in paraphenomenon?
(i.e. ESP, telekinesis, pyrokinesis, telepathy, etc.)

If you had the ability to see into the future,
would you attempt to change anything?

Perspectives on God

"The same belief in God's power to transform reality was shared as much
by Elijah Muhammad as a Muslim as it was by Booker T. as a christian."
(Na'im Akbar)

Do different religious denominations serve a different God or do they all
serve the same one? Is God without age, color, and culture?

Do you believe that God speaks to humans
as we do to one another? If not, how does God
communicate with us, or does God communicate with us at all?

Religious Worship

"He that is in you is greater than he that is in the world."
(Holy Bible—I John 4:4)

Are you comfortable talking about religion? Why or why not?

Do you think that all Blacks should belong
to one religious denomination with one leader
(Besides God of course)?

Beyond Human

*"When truth comes, falsehood vanishes, and falsehood
is forever a vanishing thing." (Holy Qu'ran)*

Do you really believe that there are alien beings on other planets?

Are flying saucers some fictional part
of someone's imagination or do they actually exist?

Do you believe ghosts exist? What about spirits?

Life & *Death*

"Something can be defined as alive if it fears its own death."
(Unknown author)

Have you ever considered being cremated as opposed to having a traditional funeral/burial arrangement?

Are you afraid of dying? Are you afraid of living?

Is a person in a coma closest to life or death?

Body Beautiful

"Beauty has a socially shared meaning, but preferences and tastes are purely individual." (R.L. Jackson, II)

If you were to get a tattoo, what kind would you get, where would you put it, and why?

Do you think you are attractive? What makes you that way?

What body part are you most attracted to in others?

Health & Nutrition

"Stop Doing. Start Being."
(Iyanla Vanzant)

Do you feel differently about overweight people
than you do underweight people?

Out of all of your favorite foods, which three negatively
effect your diet and therefore should be eliminated from your diet?

Oneness with God

"To get to a place where you can [sic] love anything you choose—not to need permission for desire—well now, that is [sic] freedom."
(Toni Morrison)

Is it possible to achieve oneness with God?

Do you think meditation brings you closer to God?

Is it possible to ever feel complete in life?

The Value of Style

*"Content is of great importance, but we must
not underrate the value of style."
(Maya Angelou)*

Do you find persons with a lot of body hair attractive?

What makes a sexy person sexy to you?

Do you find yourself most attracted to persons
who have a similar physique to yours?

Romancing the Mind

"Each of us is God's living enterprise, a physical expression of the divinity that created us.
But, our divine potential is meaningless if we are unaware of it."
(Susan Taylor)

Do you believe that God is inside every human?
If so, how do you explain evil behavior?

What would someone have to do to "sweep you off your feet" romantically?

Is there an identifiable trend in the companions
that you have chosen to date?

Emotions

"All my kidding is serious if you can read it right."
(Eric Berne)

Do you have any fears? What is one of your greatest?

What three things bring you the most joy?

What produces the most anxiety for you?

Dreams & *Recollections*

*"God makes no mistakes. In all our trials
and dramas there are lessons." (Susan Taylor)*

How do you explain coincidences?
Is this God's way of letting HIS/HER presence be known?

What is one of your fondest memories?

What dream have you had that occurs repeatedly?
(If you don't dream, what about flashbacks?)

All About You

Personal Priorities

"You will never know who you are in the world until you know thyself."
(John Henrick Clarke)

Which is first priority in your
relationships—affection, inclusion, or control?

Are you a person who requires a lot of "space" in relationships
or do you find yourself too attached to worry about space ?

Do you feel it's important to have a lot of friends, just a few, one, or none?

Self-Assurance

"If you try to cleanse others—like soap, you will waste away in the process"
(Madagascarian proverb)

Do you feel it's okay to talk to yourself? If so, when is it appropriate?

Are you actually a "people person"
or do you find yourself tense around new acquaintances?

Are you happy with your personal appearance?
If not, what are you doing to remedy the problem?

Personality Inheritance

"The fruit don't ever fall too far from the tree."
(Old wise saying—Unknown Author)

Which of your parents are you most like in mannerisms & appearance?

What characteristic have you inherited from
one of your parents, for which you are grateful?
Which one are you not so grateful for?

What one characteristic from childhood have you carried into adulthood?
and also into your personal relationships?

Self-monitoring/Criticism

"If there is no struggles there is no progress"
(Frederick Douglass)

What is your greatest attribute? Accomplishment?

What is your greatest weakness? Disappointment?

Is it easier for you criticize or praise others' behaviors?

Curiousity/Exploration

"Symbols communicate from one person's subconscious to the subconscious of another who shares the same identity and survival necessity."
(Frances Cress Welsing)

If given the opportunity to spend an evening with someone, who you've always distantly admired, what kinds of questions would you ask? Where would you take them?

Do you feel it is necessary to define who you are, what makes you "tick"?

If you were a map, what city in the U.S. would your personality represent?

Expression of Self

"The key that opens is also the key that locks."
(Guy Zona from The House of the Heart is Never Full)

Have you ever been afraid to confront authority? Explain.

Is it difficult for you to express how you feel emotionally?
Is it easier for you to
express negative emotions than positive ones?

Life Goals

"The only time success comes before work is in the dictionary"
(Patricia Russell-McCloud)

What goals/aspirations do you have in life?

Do you confront or avoid life obstacles?

If you were dying, what three things would
you want to say you accomplished in life?

Self & *Others*

"There was a door to which I found no keg. There was a veil past which I could not see."
(Omar Khayyam from the Rubaiyat)

Are you mostly selfish or self-less? Would your closest friends agree?

Are you a pretty competitive individual?
Does that carry over into your relationships? If so, how?

Have you ever considered adoption? Would you, if you haven't?

Relationship Carryovers

"Although my mother was a female, she was not a member of this silly enemy called girls."
(Bill Cosby from Love & Marriage)

Do you seek companions who personalities
are similar to one of your parent's/guardian's?

Is personal hygiene one of your top three concerns
when choosing a mate? What about top five?

Facing Yourself / Bare Truth

*"Self possession in the full sense of that expression is
the companion to self-knowledge."*
(Patricia Williams)

Are you a difficult person to get along with?

What has been your greatest challenge in life?

If you had everything you ever wanted in life,
what one thing couldn't you do without?

Self-growth

"To be unaware of one's form is to live a death."
(Ralph Ellison)

Do you believe that your overall maturity, spiritual
knowledge, and cultural consciousness increases with age?

How many books have you read this year? Were they about the same topic?

Is it possible to want youth and all its glory so much
that you never really grow up?

Spirituality / Giving

"If you seek enlightenment outside yourself, any discipline or good deed will be meaningless."
(Nichiren Daishonia from On Attaining Buddhahood)

How often do you pray, outside of "saying your blessing" at meal time?

How do you respond to strangers who ask for money?
(i.e. are you sympathetic, annoyed ... ?)

Do you see challenges as an opportunity to exercise your faith?

Knowing You

"As a man thinketh so he is."
(Holy Bible—Proverbs 4:23)

Do you consider yourself knowledgeable of current events?

If you had to sacrifice one of your five senses, which would it be and why?

What are the first three items of clothing you take off
when you get home from school/work?

Closeness of Family

*"Just as your children are not afraid to let you know that they are not perfect,
you should not be afraid to let them know that you're not perfect."*
(Bill Cosby from Fatherhood)

Is family connectedness very important to you?

How do you respond to criticism? By a family member?
By a friend? By a stranger?

Do you want to have children?

Living & Loving

"One is responsible to life....One must negotiate this passage as nobly as possible."
(James Baldwin)

Have you ever been afraid to love?

Do you find yourself reflecting on your childhood frequently?

If you had the opportunity to plan out your next life,
what would you plan to do or be?

Physical & Mental Health

"Without discipline, we can solve nothing."
(M. Scott Peck from The Road Less Traveled)

Does your diet contribute to or subtract from your health?

Do you feel annoyed, enthusiastic, or indifferent about controversy?

Identity

"Only once have I been made mute, that is when a man asked me, who are you?"
(Kahlil Gibran)

Would you consider yourself an introspective person?

Is it possible to go throughout life
without ever knowing who you really are?

If you were to parallel your life to a book, what kind of book would you be?
(e.g. horror, mystery, romance, suspense, etc.)

Soul Searching

"A hibernation is a covert preparation for a more overt action."
(Ralph Ellison)

What are two of the biggest personal criticisms your friends have of you?

Do you often feel compelled to agree with people or prove them wrong?

Love & Relationships

Defining Love

*"We must celebrate what is constant—birth, struggle, and death are constant,
and so is love, though we may not always think."
(James Baldwin)*

Is is important to you that you and your companion
share the same definition of love?

Why do you think some people think of love
as a feeling and not a process, or both?

Is there a difference between being in love and loving? Explain.

Love & Gender Roles

*"Men who already have been able to surmount strereotyped role casting and expectations....
can achieve the ultimate in the man-woman relationship."*
(Herb Goldberg from Hazards of Being Male)

Does your companion behave in ways
that are contrary to traditional gender expectations?

Within relationships, is it more acceptable
for women not to work than it is for men not to work?

Control & Dominance

"A man with too much ambition cannot sleep in peace."
(Baguirimi Proverb)

Comment on the statement, "The one
who loves the least controls the relationship"?

Should the man be the head of the household,
or is that an archaic notion?

Are relationships naturally competitive?
Does that competition lead toward abuse?

Age & Love

*"....Yet most of us are unable to develop our capacities for love on the only
level that
really counts—a love that is compounded of maturity,
self-knowledge, and courage."*
(Erich Fromm)

When considering a companion, from
which age range do you select your mate?

Do you prefer older, younger, or same-age companions?
Have you ever asked yourself why?

Is there anyone who is incapable of loving?
Is age a factor in one's capability to love?

Truth & Loyalty

"Without wood a fire goes out, without gossip a quarrel dies down"
(Holy Bible—Proverbs 26:20)

If one of your attractive subordinates at work,
aggressively pursued you, but you were already in
a committed relationship, how would you "put out the fire" ?

If you could create the perfect soul-mate that
was everything you ever wanted, would you be
happy or would you still be unfulfilled?

Do you want the truth at all times even if it costs you the relationship?

Romance & Love

"The unspoken word is born, I see it in our eyes dancing."
(Sonia Sanchez)

Describe your idea of the perfect romantic evening?

Does the definition of love vary among cultures? If so, how so?

How many ways can you tell your partner
you love him/her without speaking? List them.

Relational Issues

"No investigation, no right to speak."
(Confucius)

If a jealous acquaintance told you he/she slept
with your companion recently, would you believe?
him/her? Would you approach your companion? If so, how?

If you confided in your friend an interest in a certain person,
and then your friend pursued that
person for him/herself, what would be your response?

Doing Your Part

"Our intimate relationships hold a mirror before us, exposing a self we don't see."
(Susan Taylor from In the spirit*)*

How does your partner feel when they are around you?
What does that say about you?

Do you think that you give your companion the most that you can give?

Fear & Others

"For the victim the questions are very simple. If noone embraces, how can you embrace yourself."
(Dorisjean Austin)

Have you ever been afraid of someone who loved you? If so why?

Are there certain topics that you are uncomfortable discussing with your Companion? If so, what are they?

Attraction to Others

"Your measure of attractiveness reflects the perception you have of your own beauty."
(R.L. Jackson, II)

What attracts you initially, personality or physical appearance?
What about in the long-run?

Would you date someone who is bald? Has an Afro? Dreadlocks?
Nappy Twists?

If you were of average height, would you
date someone extremely tall or extremely short?
(The same height is not an option)

Love & Marriage

"I was married once. It was the result of a misunderstanding between myself and a young woman."
(Author unknown)

When married, do you feel it's necessary to have a hidden account?

In marriages, should all debts be shared, including ones that existed prior to the relationship?

If you were the sole provider in your marriage, would you feel obligated to equally distribute all monies?

Navigating the Limits of Love

*"Black couples tell me all the time that what their relationship desperately
needs is effective communication."*
(Aubrey Chapman)

Do you believe, with work, any relationship can be successful?

What would make you stop loving your companion?

Can one person fulfill all of your necessities in a relationship?

Interpreting Love

"Noone can figure out your worth, but you."
(Pearl Bailey)

If you had to draw a symbol of love other than a heart,
what would you draw?

Does sex bring people closer emotionally? Is sex a spiritual experience?

Where do you draw the line between sex and aggression?

Healthy Relationships

"If you always do what you always did, you will always get what you always got."
(Jackie "Moms" Mabley)

Would you recommend that all couples
seek counseling at some point in their relationship?

Do you find yourself in mostly short-term or long-term relationships?
What does that say about you? (allow at least one other person to give
their analysis after you answer the question)

Experiencing Insecurities & Inhibitions

"Men simply copied the realities of their hearts when they built prisons."
(Richard Wright)

Do you express your fears in a relationship or do you keep them to yourself? If you keep them
to yourself, do you feel you are somehow
sabotaging the relationship's success?

What kinds of secrets, if any, should be kept from your spouse?

Which is better, to get fully emotionally "naked"
with your life partner or leave a
little mystery? Is mystery important in a marriage or relationship?

Defining Boundaries

"Until you handle it with grace, it will stay in your face."
(Les Brown)

When entering a committed relationship, do you want your companion
to cut all ties with previous
intimate partners? Should they dispose
of all memorabilia from these relationships?

How do you feel about your companion having friends of the opposite sex?

If you found out that your companion
was HIV positive and there's a possibility that you may be
infected, how would you respond?
Would you maintain or terminate the relationship?

Purest Instances of Love

"This is the purest instance of love without requital:
I love the flower, not because it
blossoms for me, but because it blossoms wholly without reference to me, and
I
rejoice in its existence, not as though it were my possession."
(*Eugen Herrigel from* The Method of Zen)

If your husband/wife told you that he/she
did not want to work for the next
five years, how would you respond?

Do you expect to assist your companion in fulfilling their major
goals or is that an individual challenge?

Is true love completely unconditional or are there exceptions?
If so, what are they?

That's Deep!

Black Progress

"The harvest is past. The Summer is ended, and we are not saved."
(Holy Bible—Jeremiah 8:20)

If the U.S. government finally gave Blacks economic reparations for the holocaust of slavery, what would those reparations entail? How much money, land, etc. would be sufficient?

Do you believe that voting contributes to race progress?

Is it possible for African Americans
to construct a separate government within America?

Truth & Race Pride

"When you kill the ancestor, you kill yourself."
(Toni Morrison)

Are African Americans more African or American? If you've
never been to Africa, can you still be African?

Does it really make a difference if all Americans believe
that Africa is the cradle of civilization?

What are three of the most important things/persons/events that
you would like your child to know about his/her history?

Defining Blackness

"It is the calm and silent water that drowns a man."
(Ashanti Proverb)

Is it true that if anyone Black is in your family's lineage,
then you are Black?

What ways do Blacks pattern themselves after Whites?
What ways do Whites pattern
themselves after Blacks? Why do you suppose we do this?

True Liberation & Slavery

"It is far better to be free to govern or misgovern yourself,
than to be governed by anybody else."
(Kwame Nkrumah)

What are the first three institutions
that must be altered first in order to achieve liberation?

Do you celebrate your independence on the fourth of July?
Why or why not?

Are the following examples forms of modern-day slavery: tattoos,
brands, processed hair, body piercing, and men wearing earrings?

Black Leadership

"For unto whomsoever much is given, of him shall much be required."
(Holy Bible—Luke 12:48)

Is it better to serve or to lead the Black community?

Has the African American community ever chosen a leader,
who primarily spoke
using the language of the people (Black English), and not the language
of the establishment (standard American English)?

Is it critical for the African American community
to unanimously select one leader,
several leaders, or none at all? What should be the criteria for selecting
persons to lead the African American community?

Black Paranoia & Suspicion

".... A piece of work that will make sick men whole. But are not
some whole that we must make sick."
(William Shakespeare from Julius Caesar)

Do you believe that Black people are paranoid
about race-related issues? Explain.

Should all African Americans who are working
for the betterment of the African American community live
within a predominantly African American neighborhood?

Philosophical Issues

"Thy people shall perish from lack of knowledge."
(Holy Bible—Hosea 4:6)

Besides money and material resources (i.e. house, car, etc.),
what's the difference between being rich and poor?

Is justice always right?

Do races really exist?

Validating & Defining Others

"You must structure your world so that you are constantly reminded of who you are."
(Na'im Akbar)

Who validates your womanhood or manhood?

How is our sexuality determined?
Are people born gay or are there societal influences?

Should we redefine gender roles to further the cause of liberation?

Money & The Black Community

"Land is the basis of all economic security. Land is essential to freedom, justice, and equality. Land is true independence."
(Malcolm X)

What do you expect the collective wealth
of the Black community to be in 10 years?
Will it have increased or decreased from what it is now?

Do you think there will ever be an African American trust fund that is
financially supported by the majority of the African American community,
and managed by a few persons?

Gender & Maturity

"Black men can not easily love a Black woman when they are so unsure of their commitment and loyalty."
(Audrey B. Chapman)

Are women partially responsible for the immaturity
and irresponsibility of some Black men?

Is it true that a Good Black Man is hard to find?
What about a Good Black woman, is she also hard to find?

Education & Blacks

"I am deliberate and afraid of nothing."
(Audre Lorde from New Year's Day)

Do you think that African American scholars should conduct research on White Americans from an afrocentric perspective?

Does the talented tenth exist today?

Should Historically Black Colleges & Universities be solely supported by the African American community, and reject governmental support?

Ashes to Ashes, Beginning to End

"Something can never become nothing."
(*The* Kybalion)

Are children born innocent or with psychological disturbances that cause them to do evil early or later on in life?

If there's no life after death, explain how it is possible to communicate with the deceased?

Black Revolution

"The Black masses are crying out, "What have we to lose but our chains?"
(Malcolm X)

Should African Americans attempt to create a unified outlook
on political issues that effect African Americans?

Is it possible to remain human in the midst of so much inhumanity?

Must every revolutionary be willing
to face death in order to fight for his/her cause?

Bending the Rules

"The bell rings loudest in your own home."
(Yoruba proverb)

Should the U.S. government make exceptions to the constitution and eradicate such organizations as the North American Man/Boy Love Association and the KKK?

Should African Americans conduct private trade negotiations with African countries?

Testing the depth of language

"For it is through our names that we first place ourselves in the world."
(Ralph Ellison)

Do animals have language?

If a baby is born, and noone including yourself ever gives the baby a name, how do you relate to or refer to the baby?

Human Progress

"You must act as if it is impossible to fail."
(Ashanti Proverb)

Is the progression of African Americans detrimental
to the progression of Whites?

How do you cure an entire society that is sick?

Which will come first, a female or Black president of the United States?

Just Being You

"Under and behind all outward appearances or manifestations, there must always be a Substantial Reality"
(The Kybalion)

Can an individual exist successfully in an interracial relationship without sacrificing part or all of his/her cultural consciousness?

Is it possible to still maintain your youth
without exhibiting child-like behaviors?

What feeling do we appeal to in people to attract them to us?

About the Author

Ronald L. Jackson II is most importantly a father of two beautiful children (Niyah & Niles) and also a husband, son, brother, and son of God. Additionally, he is author of *The Negotiation of Cultural Identity* (Praeger Press) and the forthcoming *Negotiating the Black Body: intersections of identity, culture and communication* (SUNY Press). Also, he is co-author (with Michael Hecht and Sidney Ribeau) of the forthcoming second edition of *African American Communication* (Lawrence Eerlbaum Publications) as well as numerous essays written in specialized academic journals and books. He received his doctorate in intercultural communication and rhetoric from Howard University and his M.A. and B.A. degrees in organizational communication and communication studies, respectively, from the University of Cincinnati. A communication theorist, professional speaker, and cultural trainer, he specializes in the social and intellectual construction and negotiation of cultural, gender, and racial identities. Dr. Jackson continues to travel extensively throughout the United States doing motivational speeches and seminars concerning the impact of race on the identities and everyday lives of African Americans. He is presently an Assistant Professor of Culture and Communication Theory in the Department of Speech Communication at the Pennsylvania State University in University Park, Pennsylvania.